Yuri Bezmenov: The Life and Legacy of the Infl[uential...] Defected to the Wes[t]

By Charles River Editors

The KGB's emblem

About Charles River Editors

Charles River Editors is a boutique digital publishing company, specializing in bringing history back to life with educational and engaging books on a wide range of topics. Keep up to date with our new and free offerings with this 5 second sign up on our weekly mailing list, and visit Our Kindle Author Page to see other recently published Kindle titles.

We make these books for you and always want to know our readers' opinions, so we encourage you to leave reviews and look forward to publishing new and exciting titles each week.

Introduction

"The main emphasis of the KGB is not in the area of intelligence at all. Only about 15% of time, money, and manpower is spent on espionage and such. The other 85% is a slow process which we call either ideological subversion or active measures ... or psychological warfare." – Yuri Bezmenov

The KGB is one of the most famous abbreviations of the 20th century, and it has become synonymous with the shadowy and often violent actions of the Soviet Union's secret police and internal security agencies. In fact, it is often used to refer to the Soviet state security agencies throughout its history, from the inception of the inception of the Cheka (Extraordinary Commission) in 1917 to the official elimination of the KGB in 1992. Whether it's associated with the Russian Civil War's excesses, Stalin's purges, and even Vladimir Putin, the KGB has long been viewed as the West's biggest bogeyman during the second half of the 20th century.

Inevitably, some of the Cold War's most shadowy actions involved trying to turn Soviet assets, whether for propaganda or intelligence purposes, but the Soviet system constantly had to worry about defections, as evidenced by the construction of the Berlin Wall in the early 1960s. That said, while the whistleblowers may be celebrated if they damage the public relations of an adversary, they can be controversial if they damage one's own country, as evidenced by the polarizing reputations of individuals like Edward Snowden and Julian Assange.

Yuri Bezmenov was among the first Soviet whistleblowers to attract attention on a global scale, and interest in his story has recently been revived thanks to his surprising cameo in the teaser trailer for *Call of Duty Black Ops: Cold War* in August 2020. This came despite the fact he was far from the first ex-KGB agent or Russian to pull back the curtains on the Russian government and reveal the harrowing "truths" they were once sworn to harbor, as well as the disconcerting covert operations of which they once allegedly partook. In fact, the history of Russian defectors who later emerged as informants in the name of public interest stretches back to the 16th century, when Andrey Kurbsky, a former *boyar,* high-ranking military commander, and trusted adviser to Tsar Ivan the Terrible, decamped to Lithuania on April 30, 1564.

Nonetheless, Bezmenov remains known for his works after becoming disillusioned with the Soviet system in middle age, his interest in India, and his ultimate defection to Canada, which led to him railing against Soviet communism in various lectures and works throughout the 1980s.

Yuri Bezmenov: The Life and Legacy of the Influential KGB Informant Who Defected to the West chronicles how Bezmenov went from the KGB to a thunderous anti-Soviet activist in America in the 1980s. Along with pictures of important people and places, you will learn about Bezmenov like never before.

Yuri Bezmenov: The Life and Legacy of the Influential KGB Informant Who Defected to the West

About Charles River Editors

Introduction

Free Books by Charles River Editors

Discounted Books by Charles River Editors

The Inner Workings of the KGB

"I was engaged in something much more unpleasant than espionage. I was engaged in ideological subversion, which is seldom explained to people by your media, because the media is part of that process." – Yuri Bezmenov

In part because Russia was always viewed by Western Europeans as somewhat foreign and not truly European, history has no shortage of fascinating stories about Russian defections and their results. For example, when Andrey Kurbsky decamped to Lithuania and came under the protection of Sigismund II Augustus, who reigned over Lithuania and Poland, Kurbsky translated a number of Christian and classical texts, but it was his original works that thrust him into the spotlight. In the *History of the Grand Prince of Moscow*, as well as a string of letters exchanged between Kurbsky and Tsar Ivan that were later publicized, the former accused the latter of cruel despotism, moral corruption, and the unwarranted and paranoid distrust of the Russian aristocracy, which supposedly grew twofold after the untimely death of the tsar's wife. The tsar's acrimony towards the nobles was so potent that it eventually resulted in the declaration of *oprichnina*, which stripped the *boyars* of their private property and numerous other privileges, as well as the public executions of many oppressed aristocrats. Now, whether or not all of Kurbsky's claims rang true remains a matter of dispute among modern historians. Nevertheless, Kurbsky's decision to jump ship and swear allegiance to a rival flag was met with dire consequences. Not only was the renegade vilified as a traitor, his possessions were immediately seized, and his mother, wife, and child were arrested and imprisoned in the dungeons of a Moscow fortress. Legend had it that his wife died in the cell not long after of a broken heart.

Georges Sergeevich Agabekov is widely held to have been the first KGB defector to air the Soviets' dirty laundry. The former Red Army soldier and multilingual senior OGPU (the secret police force of the USSR launched in 1923 and rebranded as the People's Commissariat for Internal Affairs, or the "NKVD," in 1934) agent abandoned his glittering career, which had taken him to cities such as Tashkent, Kabul, and Tehran, and fled to Paris in the summer of 1930. Agabekov went on to pen tell-all pamphlets and autobiographical memoirs, the most notable of which was titled *OGPU: The Russian Secret Terror,* published a year after his defection.

A sketch of Agabekov

Agabekov later insisted that it was the death of democracy, as well as the party's warped sense of morality and the violent persecution (and execution) of anyone who dared to defy the state's draconian orders that impelled him to sever ties with his motherland. Some historians, however, have theorized that Agabekov's desertion had virtually nothing to do with his discontent towards Stalin's iron-fisted, authoritarian regime and more to do with an ultimatum posed by a woman whom he had fallen head over heels for: Isabel Streater, a 19-year-old Englishwoman based in Istanbul who earned a living as an English instructor. Agabekov had been under her tutelage, and the pair struck up a romantic relationship shortly after their first meeting. When Agabekov popped the question, Streater, as the story goes, agreed under the non-negotiable condition that her partner part ways with his life of espionage forever. Whatever the case, Agabekov spent the remaining seven years of his life dodging several assassination attempts until he vanished in the Pyrenees in July 1937. It is now presumed that he was murdered by vengeful NKVD agents.

Roughly a year after Agabekov's "disappearance," a Ukrainian-born Soviet "illegal resident spy" and intelligence recruiter named Walter Krivitsky boarded the *Normandie* and fled to the United States just weeks before the onset of World War II. Krivitsky, who previously worked in places such as Poland, Hungary, and Italy, where he intercepted Nazi-Japanese transmissions and nabbed blueprints for planes and submarines, carved out a name for himself as a staunch anti-Stalinist and regularly collaborated with American journalists, who deemed him a "Soviet expert" on news pieces regarding the USSR. On top of exposing the plans for the contentious Molotov-Ribbentrop Pact several months before it was scheduled to be signed, he also cooperated with the FBI, and in an interview in July 1939, he revealed that there were currently 15 undercover Soviet agents actively carrying out espionage assignments in New York City alone. Four months later, articles first published in the *Saturday Evening Post,* in which Krivitsky recounted his experiences as a Soviet agent, were compiled into a book aptly titled *In Stalin's Secret Service* and released to the masses.

Krivitsky

In early February 1941, Krivitsky checked into Washington's Bellevue Hotel under the alias "Walter Poref," and about three hours later, Krivitsky's lifeless body was discovered by one of the housekeepers, sprawled out awkwardly across the bed with a bullet lodged in his temple. Three suicide notes written in Russian, English, and German had been placed on the bedside table, and though the local authorities ruled his death a suicide, skeptics, including his lawyer Louis Waldman, claimed that Krivitsky had composed the suicide notes under duress before he was assassinated by the NKVD.

After World War II, the Soviet Union recognized the United States as its "main enemy." Great Britain, the main object of NKVD interests before the war, became a secondary concern. During the war, when the Soviet Union found itself allied with the U.S. and the British, Russian intelligence was working in the West with less interference than ever before, but once the war ended and the Cold War dawned, Moscow faced new problems. The first, oddly enough, was the demobilization of American and British intelligence units. The decision by President Truman to liquidate the Office of Strategic Services (the predecessor of the CIA) in September 1945 deprived the NKGB and many of their agents of the possibility of penetration into their main enemy's secret services. After the establishment of the Central Intelligence Agency (CIA) in 1947, Soviet intelligence had to start from scratch. Moreover, their penetration into the CIA was much more difficult than penetration into the OSS had been.

By the time the CIA was created in July 1947, many effective verification methods had become widely used that made the introduction of Soviet agents impossible. Soviet intelligence services would be able to inflict the greatest damage on American intelligence via the interception and decipherment of classified intelligence.

While Moscow retained intelligence forces in the West, the West did not have the same opportunities in Moscow. Almost all attempts to penetrate Russia across the border from the Baltic in the north and Turkey in the south failed as a result of Moscow's counterintelligence operations.

The 1950s saw the death of Stalin, the brief stay in power of Beria, the rejection of Stalin's cult of personality by Nikita Khrushchev; the first political "thaw," and the birth of the KGB. Once its structure and principles of activity were formed, it remained mostly unchanged for almost 40 years.

The situation in America had also dynamically been changed. For example, in January 1956, under President Eisenhower's direction, a Council of Consultants was formed to periodically review intelligence issues abroad, and the intelligence apparatus of England was expanded. From 1955-1957, four new departments were created to work against socialist countries. In 1957-1958, a major reorganization of intelligence and counter-intelligence bodies of France was carried out.

One of the main reasons for the reforms was the need to carry out tasks arising from the countries' membership in NATO. On a semi-legal basis, the German intelligence service "The Organization of Gehlen" was included in the structure of the government bodies of West Germany until 1956. In contrast to the first post-war decade, when West Germany had led tactical reconnaissance in Hungary, the GDR, and Czechoslovakia, it now began conducting reconnaissance operations in the territory of the Soviet Union.

After Stalin's death, there was a weakening of the repressive policy toward those who had cooperated with the German occupiers during the Great Patriotic War. In September 1955, the Decree of the Presidium of the Supreme Soviet of the USSR gave amnesty to this category of citizens. Former Soviet citizens who had found themselves abroad now returned to the country.

Between 1955 and 1958, over 12,000 people came home, and foreign special services hastened to use this "channel" to send agents to the Soviet Union. According to author Alexander Sever,

"Since 1956, among the immigrants arriving in the USSR, operational officers exposed 30 to 50 foreign intelligence agents and emissaries of anti-Soviet centers and organizations every year. In particular, in 1957, 26 agents of the imperialist intelligence services and 36 participants of foreign anti-Soviet centers and organizations were found among the arriving immigrants."

Not only did the Russian intelligence services have to fight with the external enemies of the Soviet state, they also had to deal with internal enemies, such as "Banderaers" and "forest brothers" who had cooperated with the German invaders. After the Red Army had liberated the territory of Western Ukraine, Belarus, and the Baltic States, they began to terrorize and plunder the local civilian population.

According to the Resolution of the Central Committee of the Communist Party (CPSU) of March 12, 1954, the main operational activities of state security agencies in the latter 1950s included the struggle against destructive activities of the imperialist intelligence services and foreign anti-Soviet centers, the elimination of the remnants of the "bourgeois-nationalist underground" in the territories of Western Ukraine, Belorussia, and the Baltic republics, and the struggle against anti-Soviet elements, such as churchmen, sectarians, and other hostile elements within the country (Sever, 2008). By the beginning of the 1960s, the Soviets had only managed the second task of eliminating the remnants of the "bourgeois-nationalist underground."

The 1950s were also recognized in the Soviet Union as a "period of reforms and reductions." From 1953-1967, the Soviet Union had five leaders, structural and functional changes took place regularly, and massive staff cuts were made. The Central Committee of the CPSU began the process of transforming state security on July 11, 1951, due to " the unfavorable situation in the Ministry of State Security of the USSR." Two days later, the Minister of the MGB, General Viktor Abakumov, lost his position and was arrested. He was replaced by former secretary of the Central Committee of the CPSU, Semyon Ignatiev. The change of the head of the department subsequently led to a series of resignations in the central apparatus and in territorial bodies.

In January 1952, a system of secret informants was eliminated and a new category of special agents was introduced. That November, the Bureau of the Presidium of the CPSU Central Committee also established a commission to reorganize the intelligence and counter-intelligence services of the MGB USSR. As a result of its activities, the Bureau of the Presidium of the CPSU Central Committee adopted a decision (BP7 / 12-op of December 30, 1952) for the establishment of the Main Intelligence Directorate in the USSR MGB on January 5, 1953, by the order of MGB No. 006, but the project was never implemented due to the death of Stalin in March 1953.

New reforms began after that. At a joint meeting of the Plenum of the CPSU Central Committee, the Council of Ministers of the USSR and the Presidium of the Supreme Soviet of the USSR, a decision was made to merge the MGB and Ministry of Internal Affairs (Ministry of the Interior of the USSR). This move was initiated by Beria. At the same meeting, it was decided to appoint Beria as the First Deputy Chairman of the Council of Ministers of the USSR, and at the same time, Minister of the Interior of the USSR. He held these posts for a short time before being arrested on June 26, 1953, the result of an initiative undertaken by a "group of comrades from the Politburo." Beria was shot on December 23, 1953.

After Beria's arrest, Sergei Kruglov, the new Minister of Internal Affairs, filed an official note to the "instance" (the so-called Central Committee of the CPSU) on February 4, 1954, with a proposal to establish a "Committee for State Security under the Council Ministers of the USSR." This document was discussed on February 8, 1954, at the Presidium of the Central Committee of the CPSU, and fully approved.

The Committee for State Security ("Komitet Gosudarstvennoy Bezopasnosti" in Russian), was established in accordance with the Decree of the Presidium of the Supreme Soviet of the USSR of March 13, 1954. This date is considered the official date of the KGB's birth, although the Chekists mark the holiday on December 20, the day of the Cheka's creation.

Ivan Serov was appointed the first chairman of the KGB. He had risen rapidly in his career under Stalin and Khrushchev, actively participated in the procedure of rehabilitation of victims of judicial arbitrariness, and by June 1957, had fired more than 18,000 security officers, including 40 generals.

Serov

This wave of personnel changes was completed in February 1956, when Serov "reported" the dismissal of 16,000 employees to the Central Committee of the CPSU "as politically not confiable, violators of socialist legality, careerists, morally unstable, as well as illiterate and backward workers."

The second stage of "cleansing" ended in June 1957, when another 2,000 employees of the central apparatus were dismissed from state security agencies "for violating Soviet legality, abuse of office and immoral acts." There were 48 people who held the posts of heads of departments and other higher positions. As a result, as noted in the certificate prepared by Serov for the (1957) Plenum of the Central Committee, "almost all senior officials of the central administrations, departments of the central apparatus were changed." (Lubyanka, 2003). As a result of personnel cuts, the number of State Security Committee workers decreased in 1957 by half compared to 1954. Moving forward, Serov would rely both on old Chekists and new party nominees.

Under Serov, the tasks and responsibilities of the KGB's central apparatus and its local bodies were clearly formulated:

a)   intelligence work in capitalist countries;

b)   combating espionage, sabotage, terrorist, and other subversive activities of foreign intelligence agencies, foreign anti-Soviet centers, and their agents inside the country;

c)   the struggle against anti-Soviet activities and nationalist elements within the USSR;

d)   counter-intelligence work in the Soviet Army, the Navy, GVF (Civil Air Fleet), border troops, and the troops of the Ministry of Interior in order to prevent the penetration of foreign intelligence agents and other enemy elements into their ranks;

e)   counter-intelligence work at special facilities and in the sphere of transport;

f)   state border protection of the USSR;

g)   protection of party and government leaders;

h)   organization and provision of government communications;

i)   the organization of radio-reconnaissance work; [and]

j)   [the] development of mobilization plans for the deployment of the state security organs and the military units of the Committee and the fulfilment of other assignments of the Central Committee of the CPSU and the Government of the USSR.

In this document, the rights of state security bodies were defined:

a)   to have necessary agents to conduct operational works in order to identify and suppress hostile activities directed against the Soviet Union;

b)   produce and legally establish searches, detentions and arrests of persons convicted or suspected of criminal activities;

c)   to conduct an investigation in cases of state crimes, committed by officers, sergeants, servants and workers of the KGB;

d)   to carry out special measures aimed at detecting the criminal activity of foreign intelligence agents and anti-Soviet elements;

e)   in cases of necessity, in coordination with police chiefs, to involve the police in order to ensure the fulfilment of the tasks of state security bodies;

f)   to keep operative records of state criminals and persons who are suspected of belonging to foreign intelligence agencies, participation in anti-Soviet organizations, and other hostile activities;

g)   to check the state of the encryption service and secret records management in ministries and departments, as well as subordinate enterprises and institutions;

h)   to carry out a special inspection of persons with careers in relation to state and military secrets, as well as those who go abroad and back to the USSR; [and]

i)   publish literature, training, and visual aids on matters within the competence of the Committee (Shevyakin, 2004).

Over the course of its history, the activities of the KGB were regulated by more than 5,000 different normative acts approved by the Council of Ministers of the USSR. According to contemporaries of Serov, he was an agile, proactive, hard-working person who used to demand rapid decision-making from his subordinates. He listened to the opinion of famous scientists, retained departmental patriotism, and did not allow for further reduction of the central apparatus. The main reason for his resignation from his post as chairman of the KGB on December 8, 1958, was based on his complicated relationship with the USSR's highest party leadership.

After the reorganization of the Ministry of Internal Affairs and the formation of the KGB under the Council of Ministers of the USSR, counter-intelligence was renamed the Second Main Directorate of the KGB (VGU). At that point, security officers had to completely reorganize their work. If earlier foreign secret services actively used their agents in the territory of the Soviet Union through illegal channels, now they preferred legal means of "delivering" them to the territory of the Soviet Union. Naturally, the Soviets assumed the best place to find foreign spies would be among embassy employees, tourists, journalists, and businessmen. In 1955 and the first half of 1956, the Soviets exposed more than 40 foreign spies "among American, British, French and other delegation participants."

The sphere of interests had also been changed. Now, the object of their increased attention was the sphere of nuclear energy, the creation of hydrogen weapons, and rocketry. The wide use of the latest radio electronic equipment, pulsed radio navigation, and radar devices was used. By 1956, foreign intelligence had switched to one-way radio communication with its agents. Microphotography was also widely used. A popular way of contacting agents working under diplomatic cover in the territory of the Soviet Union was the use of systems of impersonal communication. All of this greatly complicated the identification of enemy agents.

In 1954, a strengthening of the intelligence apparatus was carried out, excluding agents who did not inspire confidence and who were incapable of assisting the KGB authorities with their personal qualities and counter-intelligence capabilities. In 1955, the KGB issued Order No. 00420, "On Improving Agency Work," which aimed "to recruit persons with higher and secondary education who possessed the necessary personal qualities and operational capabilities to conduct spy and other subversive activities, to search for state criminals and solve other counter-intelligence tasks" (Abramov, 2006).

The Makings of a Puppet

"As I mentioned before, exposure to true information does not matter anymore. A person who is demoralized is unable to assess true information. The facts tell him nothing, even if I shower him with information, with authentic proof, with documents and pictures. ...he will refuse to believe it... That's the tragedy of the situation of demoralization." – Yuri Bezmenov

Despite the clear pattern that emerged with respect to the chilling fates that befell many of the Russian defectors who sought to lay bare the skeletons in the Soviets' closet, Yuri Bezmenov would consciously and unapologetically choose to throw caution to the wind, leaving behind a comfortable life and a prestigious career financed in full by the Soviet government to embark on the perilous path of a KGB whistleblower. This begs several questions, such as what was it like growing up in the so-called socialist state, how he became incorporated into the complex, insidious, and frightfully well-oiled machine that was the Soviet government, and how its cogs executive organs worked together to maintain its allegedly delusive front. Above all, many wondered why would anyone in Bezmenov's coveted position would be so resolved to "entirely disassociate [themselves]" from this formidable administration, effectively burning all bridges with his once beloved homeland.

Not surprisingly, known details of Bezmenov's childhood and formative years are sparse at best and were presumably obscured for the safety of his surviving family members, relatives, and friends back home. Yuri Alexandrovich Bezmenov was born in the Mytishchi *rayon*, situated about 20 miles northeast of Moscow in western Russia, in 1939, but his full date of birth has never been disclosed. The modest, unassuming city, now inhabited by some 204,000 citizens, was where Bezmenov spent the better part of his early childhood and adolescence. Mytischi was historically known for being a midpoint and stopping place between Moscow and the Trinity Lavra of St. Sergius – the most prominent monastery and the sacred heart of the Russian Orthodox Church – and serving as the fount of the Soviet capital's water supply until the dawn of the 1900s. By the time of Bezmenov's birth, the city had transitioned into a major manufacturing hub.

Bezmenov was undoubtedly of Russian stock, but as previously stated, the particulars surrounding the Bezmenov family tree, such as the names of his grandparents, parents, and potential siblings are unknown. The only established piece of information about Bezmenov's pedigree, which, even then, has only been mentioned in passing, was his father's profession. The senior Bezmenov was a respected, well-traveled officer of the Soviet Army General Staff, more specifically an inspector of Soviet land forces in places such as Cuba, Mongolia, Germany, and other Eastern European territories. His post, for which he was handsomely compensated, was one held in great esteem, as he was not required to answer to any middlemen and reported directly to the Minister of Defense.

Since Bezmenov's father was a high-ranking government official, he was made to toe the party line at a very early age and grew up learning heroic fables starring Lenin, Stalin, and other Bolshevik luminaries. Of course, he heard rave reviews about the administration's stellar accomplishments and contributions in general, as well as other "socialist" propaganda. Included in the stack of pictures that Bezmenov later plucked out from his photo albums before his defection was a blurry black-and-white photograph of him as a seven-year-old. Sporting what appeared to be a generic primary school uniform – a pressed collared shirt and dark neckerchief – the young Bezmenov can be seen standing next to a life-size all-white marble statue of Stalin. The lad had a blank, somewhat confused expression on his face, with slackened shoulders and one hand stiffly planted on his hip, almost as if he was oblivious to the sculpture's significance and had simply been ordered to strike a pose.

Day in and day out, Bezmenov's parents and schoolteachers alike inculcated him with the brilliance of Soviet socialism, and glorified the ultra-left wing party's meticulous plans to permanently dismantle the unjust class system, enforce laws that promoted equality across the board, and ramp up state security to protect all the citizens within the USSR.

He learned how the Bolsheviks laid the foundations of and built their socialist government from scratch. Following the Bolshevik triumph in the Russian Revolution of October 1917, the pro-capitalist Russian Provisional Government, inaugurated after the February Revolution and chaired by Alexander Kerensky, was quashed and the power transferred to the Congress of Workers', Soldiers', and Peasants' Deputies, or the "Congress of Soviets," for short. Lenin's whole campaign revolved around the previously disenfranchised working class and their best interests. The abolition of individual property, farms, factories, mines, transport firms, and other private industries – all of which were nationalized expeditiously – the party contended, meant an end to exploitation and discriminatory competition, thereby tipping the scales in the underdogs' favor. The collectivization of agriculture, leading to the creation of *kolkhozes* (collective farms) and state-owned grain stores, was vitally important, for this way, the government could keep track of every republic's food supply and ensure that all mouths were fed.

Notwithstanding all the pleasant newspeak and rose-colored communist ideology that he was constantly spoonfed, the adult Bezmenov was adamant that his father had been a true-hearted patriot through and through. The senior Bezmenov always toed the party line and had never dreamt of flouting direct orders. At the same time, he allowed himself to quietly entertain any misgivings he had about certain hard-line policies – he was, for instance, a proponent of minimizing military might – and judiciously shared his concerns with his superiors on occasion. Ultimately, however, he was aware of the prevailing circumstances and the limited extent of his influence, so he mostly continued to promote the party's ideals.

While Bezmenov's father was not necessarily the greatest fan of the Bolshevik brand of socialism, he firmly believed that the system as a whole was the key to the guaranteed welfare and prosperity of his darling native country, and he focused on the bigger picture. As such, the younger Bezmenov was taught to respect the Soviet flag and appreciate the honor that it was to be employed in any governmental sector. In the same breath, he was also taught the value of cautious optimism and was encouraged to question everything around him within reason. Most importantly, he was taught to always do what he believed was right.

Admittedly, Bezmenov could never relate to the trials, hardships, and crackdowns that many, particularly in the peasantry (stigmatized as *kulaks*), faced behind the scenes. In fact, he only benefited from Soviet communism. The Bezmenovs were by no means filthy rich, but they lived in relative luxury, as the better part of the family's bills and expenses were footed by the government, residing in an inviting, spacious manor that was abundantly furnished and boasted fully-stocked ice boxes and cupboards.

All things considered, there was nothing out of the ordinary about Bezmenov's childhood. He was a well-disciplined, straight arrow of a lad who kept his distance from other troublemakers his age, diligently kept up with his schoolwork, and treated all authority figures with due respect. As devoted as the young Bezmenov was to the revered Red Banner, however, he could not shake the feeling that something was amiss, and while these sneaking suspicions were infrequent, they were, more significantly, recurrent.

Throughout Stalin's reign, the state trumpeted the merits of their collectivization policies, which leveled the playing field for all farmers and helped nourish the growing urban workforce, allowing for the rapid industrialization of the Soviet republics. Moreover, the state bragged about the tremendous breakthroughs made by local agriculturalists and their supposed investment in superior, ultra-sophisticated agrotechnology, which enabled the authorities to keep the state food stores filled to capacity consistently. The state occasionally acknowledged the ongoing food scarcity issue that loomed over the republics for decades, but refused to label it a crisis, assuring the public that it was all under control and that there was plenty of food to go around.

Given that the Bezmenov family and their neighbors never missed a meal, the young man never felt the need to question the government's stance on the subject. That was – until he noticed the barrenness of the state grain stores firsthand. It was only in his late adolescence that he learned of the bleak reality of the USSR's severely deficient food supply, and was both horrified and ashamed of his ignorance to the unimaginable plights that millions outside of his bubble were forced to endure. He was particularly dismayed by his blindness to the Holodomor – the worst party-induced famine in Soviet history – that wreaked irreparable havoc to the Ukrainian rural population, claiming anywhere between 3.9 to 10 million lives, less than a decade before his birth. Still, Bezmenov, who was raised to believe that the party had only its citizens' best interests at heart, attempted to rationalize the authorities' censorship of these famines in the domestic and international media. He chalked up the government's determination to control the narrative to a necessary evil, perhaps aiming to avoid mass panic and unrest.

Bezmenov recalled another instance in which his faith in the authorities was put to the test. In the early 20th century, it appeared that a promising friendship had blossomed between Russia and the United States. The Americans initially nursed a grudge against the Soviet leaders for withdrawing Russia from the First World War shortly after the outbreak of the October Revolution, but the Americans seemingly buried the hatchet and extended a helping hand via a famine relief program in the USSR in the 1920s. Herbert Hoover, who was later elected the 31st president of the United States, had been assigned by President Harding to spearhead the program, for which he was allotted a hefty budget of $20 million. American entrepreneurs such as Henry Ford and Armand Hammer also helped to boost the Soviet Union's floundering economy by partnering with Russian firms during the New Economic Policy era, and the two nations officially forged diplomatic relations in 1933.

Hoover

Their relations were further strengthened when they joined forces in World War II in a triumphant bid to conquer the Nazis. The Bezmenovs themselves had reaped the fruits of Uncle Sam's generosity during the Second Great War, and he later wrote, "As a war-time child, I survived partly thanks to such 'decadent capitalist'...things as 'Spam' meat, condensed milk, and egg powder that were supplied to my country by the USA through the lend-lease program of World War II." Through the Lend-Lease Plan, the Soviet military was also gifted a total of 400,000 combat trucks, 14,000 airplanes, 13,000 tanks, and 8,000 tractors, as well as 15 million pairs of army boots, 2.7 million tons of petroleum, 4.5 million tons of food, 1.5 million blankets, and 107,000 tons of cotton.

In the wake of World War II, America was discredited as a disgraceful and aggressive champion of toxic imperialism and pronounced a sworn enemy of the USSR almost overnight. The party did not take kindly to the Western democracies' unsolicited commentary on the Soviet quest to gain control of Poland, Latvia, Estonia, and other Eastern European states, particularly President Harry Truman's vocal opposition to the Russian troops stationed in Iran and their obsession with subjugation. Winston Churchill famously portrayed the Soviet sphere of influence as an "Iron Curtain" actively seeking to reverse its transparency with the free world. Stalin retaliated by singling out "capitalist imperialism," and in effect, the United States, as the primary cause of World War II.

A series of propaganda posters circulated during the Cold War, beginning in earnest in 1947 and dedicated to promoting anti-American messages. Bezmenov came across these posters on a daily basis, as they were plastered on walls and poles, as well as the doors and windows of shopfronts and other establishments all around town. One such poster featured a scowling American soldier wielding a bloody bayonet, set amidst an ominous red and black background. It bore the following caption: "The US Army is an instrument of aggression and robbery." Another poster, which is split down the middle, features two similar, yet pointedly contradictory scenes. On one side, there is a young, well-groomed soldier engaged in a civil conversation with an elderly, modest-looking working man; this scene is juxtaposed with an overweight, snooty-looking businessman with a cigar hanging from his lips seemingly conspiring with an equally arrogant military general with a supercilious smirk. The caption for this poster reads, "Two worlds – two plans: We spread life, [and] they sow death." A third caricature, no caption needed, shows a trio of obese, scowling businessmen – two dressed in ill-fitting, yet expensive suits and monocles to match, and the third in an Uncle Sam costume – seated in thrones, indifferent to the sea of cadaverous, ashen-faced people underneath them, their skeletal arms outstretched in desperate longing.

The Bolsheviks also lambasted the United States for their hypocrisy, most markedly their deplorable oppression of black Americans and other minorities. When Orval Faubus, the governor of Arkansas, mobilized the National Guard in September 1957 in response to a group of nine black students trying to integrate the all-white Central High School in Little Rock, the Soviet newspaper *Izvestia* was quick to criticize the "facade of so-called American democracy."

An excerpt from the newspaper told readers, "The patrons of Governor Faubus...who dream of nooses and dynamite for persons with different-colored skins, advocates of hooliganism who throw rocks at defenseless Negro children – these gentlemen have the audacity to talk about 'democracy' and speak as supporters of 'freedom'." The *Komsomolskaya Pravda*, the official publication of the USSR's communist youth organization, ran a similarly provocative story, complete with photographs, with the following headline: "Troops Advance Against Children!"

From a child's viewpoint, Bezmenov was taken aback by the sudden onslaught of anti-American sentiment sweeping through the USSR, but he saw no reason to swim against the tide. There was, however, one particular point in time that led him to question the party's motives behind the wave of anti-Americanism, and also the credibility of Soviet spokespersons and domestic journalists. Bezmenov and his schoolmates were made to believe that the CIA had been air-dropping Colorado beetles – tiny, yellow and black ten-striped pests that fed on spuds – on Russian, German, and Polish potato fields, reportedly one of the Americans' slow-burn strategies to capture and occupy Mother Russia. Ivan Benediktov, the Minister of Agriculture of the USSR, warned, "American candidates for atomic war criminals today showed a sample of what they are preparing for humanity. Only murderers can resort to such horror as the deliberate destruction of peaceful human labor, the destruction of the crop by the Colorado potato beetle."

Bezmenov recalled one of his teachers distributing notebooks with a drawing of the Colorado beetle printed onto the back pages at the beginning of the school year. After school each day, Bezmenov and the boys in his class were tasked with scouring the potato fields of nearby collective farms for these wretched pests. Neither Bezmenov nor his friends were successful in snagging even a single beetle, and yet the Americans were almost entirely blamed for the spud shortage.

Even with all these glaring red flags, Bezmenov held fast to the party line and sought to "inherit" the governmental careers of the family patriarchs, dutifully continuing down the path that had been paved for him well before his birth. In 1956, 17-year-old Bezmenov was enrolled in the Institute of Oriental Languages, a school affiliated with Moscow State University and administered by the Communist Party Central Committee. The Institute, the largest and most prestigious language-learning center within the USSR, originated as the Asiatic Museum, inaugurated in November 1818 in Saint Petersburg by Count S. Uvarov, president of the Imperial Academy of Sciences. The museum was a treasure trove of Oriental and rare Muslim manuscripts, treatises centered on the histories and different cultures of the East, and priceless relics sourced from various regions and eras. In addition to serving as an exhibition space and a well-guarded repository for these irreplaceable tomes and artifacts, the museum doubled as a scholastic library and research facility. The museum's proprietors also issued its own academic journal in the French language entitled *Melanges asiatiques*, or *Asian Notes*. The Bolsheviks officially converted the museum to a language school shortly after the 1917 Revolution. Their chief objective was to educate young Russians in the history, languages, and traditions of Eastern countries and to dispatch these graduates to their respective countries of expertise, where they were instructed to promote the party's socialist ideology.

Of course, the party drew a thick veil over their plans to infiltrate other nations with their fresh batches of green, but eager overseas KGB agents. Bezmenov himself was believed to have been prepping for a postgraduate volunteer mission to harvest grain in Kazakhstan. Once again, Bezmenov was bewildered by the government's immoderate inclination to secrecy, but ultimately decided that such concerns were outside of his purview and carried on with his studies. In another photograph taken from a family album, Bezmenov, clad in a bulky black coat and a matching fur *ushanka*, can be seen standing in front of the Institute, his shoulders pulled back and the corners of his lips slightly curled upward, exuding a quiet sense of achievement.

Bezmenov was a studious student and spent most of his evenings burning the midnight oil instead of socializing with his fellow classmates throughout his seven years at the Institute. Like other standard universities, the curriculum assigned to Bezmenov consisted of literature, history, philosophy, music, and introductions to the most widely spoken Eastern tongues. His principal studies, equivalent to a college major, were centered on Indian culture. By the end of his scholarship, he had mastered several Indian languages and was a veritable expert on Indian customs and traditions. He was also well-versed in a number of classical Indian musical instruments, such as the sitar.

In contrast to many of his contemporaries, who cobbled together the bare minimum required for a diploma, Bezmenov was truly enamored by the rich and colorful heritage of India. He was fascinated with the diverse pantheon of Hindu deities, as well as the rise and fall of Indian empires throughout the years, from the Kushanas and the Guptas to the Mughal reign. He was also an Indian literature buff, and he was especially moved by the works of Acharya Hemachandra, a prolific Jain poet and polymath famed for his manuscripts on grammar, philosophy, and contemporary history, as well as the mononymous Bhartrhari, the illustrious Sanskrit author of *Satakatraya,* a compilation of poems about "moral values," and the *Vakyapadiya,* a treatise on grammar and linguistic philosophy.

आचार्य हेमचन्द्र

[वि. सं. १२९४ की ताड़पत्र-प्रति के आधार पर]

A medieval drawing of Hemachandra

Bezmenov was blown away by the subtle progressiveness of Indian culture and the understated modernity of Indian architecture and technology. The 8,000-year-old prehistoric settlements of the Indus River Valley, mostly concentrated in present-day Pakistan and western India, with a staggering population of 5 million at its height, is believed to be among the oldest and largest of the four ancient civilizations, alongside Egypt, Mesopotamia, and China. Archaeological excavations conducted in Harappa and Mohenjo-daro, the two most prominent cities in the valley, revealed systematically planned networks of wide, linear streets flanked by brick houses, and complex sewer systems, a striking inverse of the Russians' prehistoric ancestors, who were still subsisting on raw meat and residing in caves. Bezmenov was struck by the multitude of inventions and innovations attributed to Indian scientists, among which included the number zero, the concept of cataract surgery, which was developed as early as the 3rd century CE, and the cure for leprosy through the use of ancient remedies found in the *Atharva Veda,* a Vedic-era collection of scriptures and charms.

Every student, whatever their major, was also required by Soviet law to complete extensive military and civil defense training, the party's goal being to assemble a strong reserve army that could be immediately mobilized whenever necessary. All students were awarded the rank of junior lieutenant upon graduation, and Bezmenov, who achieved this title with flying colors, specialized in espionage, as well as administrative and military intelligence. During his second year, Bezmenov's professors pushed him to dress up in traditional Indian attire. In another photograph taken from his time at the Institute, Bezmenov is wearing a striped *dhoti* and a white, loose-fitting turban. Students were encouraged to adopt the fashion of the countries they specialized in, where they would be employed as diplomats and foreign journalists, to prevent culture shock.

In reality, the Institute – which Bezmenov later described as an elaborate front for a spy school – was coaching them on how to best blend in with (in Bezmenov's case) the Indian population without attracting any unwanted attention. He was trained in the ancient Russian art of *maskirovka,* meaning "something masked," a strategy of camouflage and deception employed as early as 1380, when Prince Dmitry Donskoy and his regiment of 60,000 Russian warriors lay in wait in the shadows of a dense forest for hours before ambushing and massacring the Golden Horde, an army of 150,000 Tatar-Mongolian soldiers, in what is now referred to as the Battle of Kulikovo. Contrary to popular belief, the Soviets had no delusions about their strengths and capabilities. Like Prince Donskoy, they were fully aware of the superior weapons, manpower, and overall military prowess of rival countries, and they relied on trickery and subterfuge, such as exaggerating the size of their troops and actively spreading *dezinformatsiya* (disinformation), to keep their enemies at bay.

Bezmenov was obligated to participate in *kommand- stabnii uchiniye,* which translates to "staff training activities." Participants, split into teams, were provided with actual foreign maps and presented with tactical, operational, and strategic scenarios. In a nutshell, teams were expected to devise cooperative strategies, draw up combat game plans, expand on their improvisational skills, issue directives, and exercise control on the spot. Strategies formulated by winning teams were then analyzed at length by teams of researchers on standby, some of which were integrated into the war plans of the Red Army.

War games and rigorous daily drills aside, Bezmenov and his peers underwent comprehensive training on interrogation methods and torture tactics used on political prisoners and *gulag* captives. There were reportedly 52 forms of torture inflicted upon said prisoners, which included sleep deprivation, regular beatings, and the abominable "Sukhavana Swallow," wherein, as detailed by historian Lidia Golovkova, "inmates were trussed up with a long towel that was forced between their lips like a horse's bridle, and then pulled down behind them and tied under their feet." Russian interrogation methods pivoted on the dehumanization and severe psychological manipulation of their victims. Prisoners being questioned were usually made to sit on the leg of a tipped stool for hours on end, and one false move led to immediate penetration.

Victims were also often made to soil themselves and forced to consume their own feces, which, as explained by Ruxxandra Cesereanu, author of *Portrait of the Torturer in the 20th Century*, caused them to "regress to an infantile stage, that of the child who was harshly punished by its father."

The Final Straw

"You only realize something is happening in countries when you see troop movements or shots are fired. Everything that went on before this you never hear about it." – Yuri Bezmenov

Bezmenov, who was 24 at the time of his graduation from the Institute, was perturbed by the barbarity of the interrogation and torture tactics that he picked up during his compulsory military and civil defense training, and he was equally unsettled by the patent flaws in the Soviet administrative system. Be that as it may, the buoyant enthusiasm of the bright-eyed graduate, who was ready to take on adulthood, remained wholly intact. He ascribed his concerns to his naive idealism and inexperience with the real world, and he maintained his faith in the Soviet authorities. His optimism was bolstered by what historians now call the "Khrushchev Thaw."

Beginning in October 1955, Khrushchev began to fight to tell delegates to the upcoming 20th Party Congress about the abuses of the former ruler. He received opposition, particularly from Molotov and Malenkov, but Khrushchev persisted. The other leaders finally agreed, but they got Khrushchev to agree to give his remarks to a closed session.

The 20th Party Congress opened on February 14, 1956. Khrushchev opened with remarks that contained veiled criticisms of Stalin. Nothing more was said concerning Stalin, however, until the end of the Congress. In the early morning of February 25, Soviet delegates were told to attend a special early morning closed session of the Congress; foreign reporters and observers from Communist Parties in other nations were excluded. What occurred over the next four hours was a speech by Khrushchev entitled On the Cult of Personality and Its Consequences. It became known to history as the "Secret Speech."

Before a shocked audience, Khrushchev systematically demolished Stalin's reputation. He began by stating unequivocally that there was no question about the late ruler's contributions in the Revolution, the Civil War, and in building up the economic system of the Soviet Union. But, he went on to say, a cult of personality had built up around Stalin, aided and abetted by Stalin himself; such a personality cult violated the very principles of Marxist-Leninism. From there, he moved to Lenin's own statements on Stalin: "[Lenin] detected in Stalin in time those negative characteristics which resulted later in grave consequences. Fearing the future fate of the party and of the Soviet nation, VI Lenin made a completely correct characterization of Stalin. He pointed out that it was necessary to consider transferring Stalin from the position of general secretary because Stalin was excessively rude, did not have a proper attitude toward his comrades, and was capricious and abused his power."

Khrushchev described the way in which Stalin proceeded to consolidate his power after Stalin's death: "Stalin acted not through persuasion, explanation and patient cooperation with people, but by imposing his concepts and demanding absolute submission to his opinion. Whoever opposed these concepts or tried to prove his [own] viewpoint and the correctness of his [own] position was doomed to removal from the leadership collective and to subsequent moral and physical annihilation. This was especially true during the period following the 17th party congress, when many prominent party leaders and rank-and-file party workers, honest and dedicated to the cause of communism, fell victim to Stalin's despotism."

While Khrushchev granted that Stalin did put down genuine threats to Marxism-Leninism in the Soviet Union (such as followers of Trotsky), he pointed out that once such threats had been dealt with, Stalin soon turned his sights "against many honest communists, against those party cadres who had borne the heavy load of the civil war and the first and most difficult years of industrialization and collectivization, who had fought actively against the Trotskyites and the rightists for the Leninist party line."

Stalin originated the concept "enemy of the people." This term automatically made it unnecessary that the ideological errors of a man or men engaged in a controversy be proven. It made possible the use of the cruelest repression, violating all norms of revolutionary legality, against anyone who in any way disagreed with Stalin, against those who were only suspected of hostile intent, against those who had bad reputations. The concept "enemy of the people" actually eliminated the possibility of any kind of ideological fight or the making of one's views known on this or that issue, even [issues] of a practical nature. On the whole, the only proof of guilt actually used, against all norms of current legal science, was the "confession" of the accused himself. As subsequent probing has proven, "confessions" were acquired through physical pressures against the accused. This led to glaring violations of revolutionary legality and to the fact that many entirely innocent individuals - [persons] who in the past had defended the party line - became victims.

Along with the speech, this was a period encompassing the mid-1950s to the mid-1960s, beginning right after Stalin's death, during which a number of stringent restrictions under the previous regime – namely press and media censorship, international trade, and so on – were alleviated. Peasants, who had been relentlessly denigrated and subjected to violent oppression by Stalin and his Kremlin cronies, were given passports and legal identification cards, thereby granting them their long-awaited right to evacuate their poverty-stricken villages and relocate to more prosperous metropolises. Khrushchev also green-lit the construction of *khrushchyovkas,* or affordable housing units in the form of brick or concrete apartment buildings, to accommodate the influx of new lower-class residents.

Still, it would not take long for the young Bezmenov to realize that the USSR, in his own words, was "millions [of] times more oppressed than any colonial or western power in the world," and that almost everything that he had been taught to believe by the leaders of his precious homeland were manufactured fables and fictions designed to fuel the party's underhanded schemes.

Once Bezmenov secured his diploma in 1963, he was sent to India to work as a translator and public relations officer for Soviet Refineries Constructions, an aid agency that erected crude oil refinery plants in Gujarat and Bihar. The Soviets were perfectly suited for such an undertaking, as they were said to have been the most prolific producer of energy resources in the world, retaining this title all the way up to the 1980s. This extension of Soviet support was not an isolated incident.

When India declared itself an independent nation on August 15, 1947, the leaders of the newly sovereign democratic republic scrambled to achieve and preserve their economic self-sufficiency, which they felt could best be attained through the expansion of their heavy industry sector. Their Soviet allies, whom they formally established diplomatic ties with just a month and two days before they gained sovereignty, were quick to step up to the plate by proceeding to pour millions into Indian heavy machinery, energy production, steelworks, and mining industries. As a matter of fact, it was the Soviets who helped finance half of the 16 heavy industry projects rolled out in India's second Five Year Plan.   In the following excerpt, extracted from Bezmenov's *Love Letter to America,* he attempts to make sense of India's supposed gullibility and the source of their "blind faith" in their Soviet allies: "Is it that the Indians are stupid, ignorant people, that they allow the Soviets to deceive them in this manner? On the contrary – for the most part, they are innocent victims of one of the world's most sophisticated con games: ideological subversion. They have been psychologically manipulated through media, politics, etc. into believing that the Soviets are their friends who are protecting them from the 'Western imperialists.'"

It was towards the beginning of his first legitimate job that he became acquainted with a young Indian woman who lived near his place of employment. He fell head over heels in love with the sweet maiden in a matter of weeks, entranced by her razor-sharp wit, great sense of humor, and strong, yet delicate features. Unable to bear the thought of losing her, Bezmenov popped the question, but much to his dismay, his superiors were anything but thrilled for him. Quite the opposite, they ordered him to break off the engagement at once and insisted that he find himself a nice Russian girl instead, so as to "not contaminate his genes." Bezmenov protested and defended his love for his Indian sweetheart, but all his efforts were futile. He ultimately capitulated to his superiors, and under the recommendation of the Department of Personnel, he wedded a Russian girl who had recently completed her studies in India.

Although both Bezmenov and his bride were of the same age and shared similar upbringings, it was anything but a match made in heaven. He apparently detested his new wife with a burning passion, so much so that he filed for divorce shortly after his plane touched down in Moscow two years later.

His superiors' strange, line-crossing fixation with his love life obviously had nothing to do with Bezmenov's welfare or personal contentment. All Soviet agents based abroad, Bezmenov later learned, were pressured into marriage and starting a family as soon as possible because the agent's wife and children, who were made to return to the motherland, could be used as a kind of insurance that anchored them to Russia. Agents deemed disloyal or disobedient, or even found guilty of contemplating defection, were thus risking the safety of their loved ones back home.

Bezmenov later married a second Russian girl and fathered at least one child with her – a son – and while he wasn't completely put off by his second spouse, the couple had incompatible personalities and ambitions, and they eventually separated. He later characterized his failed marital unions as "marriages of convenience." In such marriages, affection, devotion, and other traditional ingredients of a healthy, committed relationship were irrelevant. They were simply paired together so that they could keep tabs on one another, and if their partner was caught infringing on state laws, neither of them would hesitate to hand the perpetrator over to the Soviet authorities.

Following Bezmenov's two-year stint as a translator and PR officer, as previously established, he was summoned back to Moscow. He was recruited by the newly-formed Novosti Press Agency (APN), a public information service jointly founded by the Znanie (Knowledge Society), the USSR Writers' Union, Journalists' Union, and the Union of Soviet Societies for Friendship and Cultural Relations With Foreign Countries in 1961. According to *The Great Soviet Encyclopedia* (1979), the APN was created for the purpose of "[aiding] the development and strengthening of mutual understanding, confidence, and friendship among peoples." Bezmenov, however, later referred to it as "the biggest and most powerful propaganda, espionage, and ideological front of the KGB." The APN was, for lack of a better term, the central processing unit, or the "brains" of the Soviet propaganda machine, as its primary function was to compose data and compile pre-approved "facts" regarding domestic current affairs and policies, which were then passed onto local news agencies, radio and television stations, and publishing houses. Likewise, the APN filtered international news reports written by the foreign press before relaying the modified, and sometimes thoroughly altered information to local media firms.

Bezmenov was hired as an apprentice for Novosti's Political Publications (GRPP) department and was placed under the supervision of a decorated Chicago-born colonel and former foreign intelligence officer named Norman Borodin. Although the directors of Novosti never openly acknowledged the state security arm's deep-seated involvement in APN, the astute apprentice connected the dots on his own. "I [soon] discovered that about 75% of Novosti's staffers were actually KGB officers," Bezmenov later reflected. "The other 25% were 'co-optees,' or KGB freelance writers, PR officers, [and] informers like myself."

Bezmenov, who had developed quite an avid interest in writing, was disappointed to find that Novosti never published their own hard news stories, much less any serious investigative reports. Their only original pieces were human interest features and other trivial articles. Given Bezmenov's exceptional knowledge of all things Indian, he was tasked with penning puff pieces that promoted Indo-Soviet relations. For example, one of his first assignments was to cover the grand opening of an exhibition dedicated to Indian dolls and puppets at the Museum of Oriental Cultures in Moscow.

After covering a number of public relations events, diplomatic conferences, and other similar functions, Bezmenov noticed that the "official guests" invited by the state were always confined to the same group of people who either attended these gatherings together or appeared in rotation. Some of the resident guests included a Dr. Balabushevich, whom he called an "illiterate professor of Indian languages"; a well-mannered, charming diplomat named Igor Boni who was stationed in Bombay for several years; and Irina Ershova, a high-ranking member of the USSR-India Friendship Society who was little more than a pretty face and was most likely only invited to these gatherings for publicity purposes.

When Bezmenov wasn't cranking out puff pieces or translating propaganda articles, he served as a personal escort and tour guide for foreign journalists, politicians, professors, entrepreneurs, and other intellectuals and influential people who were invited to partake in international conferences in USSR locales on Novosti's dime. Unbeknownst to these people, these tours were exhaustively planned and painstakingly choreographed. Each and every one of the locals that these guests came across on every stop had been cast weeks or even months in advance, and all interactions with the locals were scripted from start to finish.

Through it all, guests were shielded from the grim realities of life in Soviet Russia and were instead infamously given tours of *potemkin* villages, otherwise known as "model villages," in Moscow and Siberia. Upon their arrival at what the guides called a "typical" collective farm, tour groups were greeted by young, burly, and affable farmers dressed in aged, but clean and well-fitting overalls with clean-shaven faces and a healthy, olive-toned tan. Oftentimes, guests were also taken to a state-owned dairy farm around the corner, where a gaggle of giggling, bubbly milkmaids in flowing white dresses and frilly aprons with rolled-up sleeves and linen bonnets awaited them. In similar fashion, tour groups in Siberia were welcomed by local Yupik Eskimos clad in their most ornate traditional parkas and most exquisite jewelry, who performed customary dances and musical performances for their guests in gorgeous snow-covered clearings of enchanting boreal forests. All of these locals, of course, spoke flawless English.

In hindsight, the kindergartens in Siberian *potemkin* villages were perhaps the most disturbing feature of these "package tours." Chubby, rosy-cheeked children with fresh crew cuts and big bows in their hair, garbed in smart uniforms and red neckerchiefs, waved at the guests with sunny smiles on their faces as they played amongst themselves in the courtyards and playgrounds. In actuality, the swing sets, seesaws, and roundabouts in these playgrounds were props that had been set up just mere days before the guests' arrival.

Bezmenov, who was fully aware of what was going on, later lamented, "What these idiots didn't understand was that it was not a kindergarten at all. It is a prison for children of political prisoners...there was not a single mention that what they were visiting [was] actually...a concentration camp. And it was the job of people like myself to help them not to notice that they are actually talking to prisoners...Of course, there were no corpses on the ground...[nor] machine gun guards...[and these places] obviously do not create an impression that they are actually prisons...And we maintain that illusion in their minds...But deep inside, I still hoped that at least some of these [guests] would understand that what they are looking at has nothing to do with the level of affluence in my nation..."

Bezmenov himself, like the other KGB-recruited tour guides, was assigned a role to play. He presented himself as a worldly, deeply knowledgeable, and sociable, yet mellow and dependable individual. While he was well-acquainted with the history and customs of his guest's country of origin and always carried himself like a solid professional – one who could set them up with powerful Soviet politicians at a moment's notice if needed – he made his charges comfortable by slipping sarcastic, but harmless quips about his own government into conversation. He was also not opposed to adding in some light hedonism.

Gaining the trust of his guests was crucial, as this helped to ensure that the next indoctrination phase of the tour could be completed without a hitch. Following the excursion to the *potemkin* villages, Bezmenov shepherded his guests to the meeting hall at the Novosti headquarters, where guests, who had already been handed a tumbler of vodka or some other cocktail upon their arrival at the Moscow Airport, received fresh alcoholic drinks that were continuously topped off throughout the day and given imported cigars and silver trays laden with *dahi vada, pani-puri, khandvi,* a wide selection of kebabs, and other delectable Indian snacks. In short, the guests were deliberately kept in an inebriated state throughout the duration of their stay, which, on average, lasted anywhere between 15-20 days.

Needless to say, Bezmenov and his Soviet colleagues made certain to remain as sober as a judge, which was achieved with the help of sobering capsules, secretly replacing their glasses of vodka with water, and pouring out their alcoholic beverages in plants and hidden canisters, among other techniques. The guests were gradually weaned off the booze towards the end of their trip. Those who visibly exhibited the worst signs of alcohol withdrawal – severe nausea, vomiting, crippling headaches, heightened anxiety, and trembling hands – were singled out by Bezmenov and his comrades since they were deemed the most "vulnerable," and therefore susceptible to manipulation. As instructed, he approached these impressionable individuals and engaged them in conversation under the guise of concern for their welfare, during which he gently coaxed them into cooperating with the KGB in terms of propaganda dissemination. These visitors believed themselves to be honorable and distinguished figures who had been invited on account of their prestige, but they were in reality, as Bezmenov crudely put it, merely "political prostitutes" who were being wined and dined so that they could be puppeteered by the Soviet administration.

The ideal guest, according to Bezmenov, was a jaded, greedy, self-absorbed character – usually academics, celebrities, and conservative journalists – who "lacked moral principles" and were willing to sell out their countries in return for money, special treatment, and shallow luxuries. They were, however, disposable pawns at best. Bezmenov explained, "When their job is completed, they are not needed anymore. They know too much. Some get offended when Marxists-Leninists come to power because they hoped they [too] would come to power. That will never happen. They will [instead] be lined up against the wall and shot...We are a bunch of murderers. There is nothing to do with friendship and understanding between the nations...We behave like a bunch of thugs [with the representatives of a] country that is hospitable to us."

Among the names in Bezmenov's lengthy list of charges was Sumitranandan Pant, one of the most renowned award-winning Indian poets of the 20th century. Pant was a great admirer of Soviet leaders and the Communist Party's socialist ideology, particularly Marx and Lenin, whose names and ideas were referenced in such poems as "*Yugvani*" and "Rhapsody to Lenin." Another guest in Bezmenov's care was Raj Kapoor, a then-obscure filmmaker who later became a celebrated director, producer, and star of the Bollywood silver screen. Despite Kapoor's unparalleled fame in his native country, Bezmenov despised him and described him as "a vulgar and trivial profiteer." He also entertained Satyajit Ray, a music composer, writer, illustrator, and motion-picture director who went on to direct 36 well-received shorts, feature films, and documentaries in his career.

A commemorative stamp of Pant

Kapoor

Propaganda preparation and tour guiding aside, Bezmenov was entrusted with attending and covering the press conferences held for the state's Indian guests. Kumaraswami Kamaraj, the founder and president of the Indian National Congress Party who arrived in Moscow in July 1966, was easily the most important name on the list. It was one of, if not the most anticipated visit of the year, as Kamaraj was at one point slated to win the seat of prime minister, only to turn it down due to his non-proficiency in Hindi and English. He did, however, play a key part in bringing two prime ministers to power: Lal Bahadur Shastri and Indira Gandhi, the first and only female Indian PM in history, which is why he was affectionately known as the "Kingmaker" of Indian politics.

A commemorative stamp of Kamaraj

The press conference was scheduled for July 30th in the glamorous grand hall of the Metropol Hotel. It was a dazzling red-carpet occasion attended by local politicians, academics, and other bigwigs, along with both foreign and domestic media personnel, and of course, the guest of honor and his cortege – all of whom were dressed to the nines. Bezmenov was stunned by the extravagance of the pageantry, considering the actual event's lack of substance and depth.

Kamaraj and his handlers did not appear the least bit confused by the reporters' suspiciously elementary non-questions; in fact, he seemed to have expected the effortless line of questioning.

His longer-form answers, which felt rehearsed, were also uncannily flattering to the Soviet Union and the Kremlin's foreign policy. As it turns out, the seemingly stilted exchange felt forced because it was precisely that because none of the reporters had prepared their own questions; each had received a unique series of questions that had been assembled for them by Novosti before the conference. Bezmenov had been instructed to inquire about the "positive effect of the spirit of the Indo-Pakistani peace conference of Tashkent [regarding] the establishment of stability and mutual security on the Indian subcontinent." All he had to do was grab a few soundbites and insert them into a template of the press conference article, which had been typed out several weeks in advance.

At the end of the day, as cushy as his job was, it wasn't always a bed of roses. His least favorite part of the job was the calculated character assassination of the bold men and women who attempted to shine a light on the Kremlin's nefarious activities. Bezmenov was personally involved in the manufacturing of the smear campaign against Deputy Prime Minister and Minister of Finance Morarji Desai, who had committed the Soviet sin of joining and later leading the Indian National Congress (Organization), the rival faction of Gandhi's Indian National Congress (Ruling), which diverged in 1969. In the months that followed, Novosti-funded newspapers, magazines, and tabloids in the "leftist liberal media" dragged Desai's name through the mud, labeling him an unprincipled "fascist," an "ultra-right-wing fanatic," and a "lackey of Western imperialism," and apart from the baseless epithets, further tarnished his reputation with spurious factoids and unfounded rumors.

Desai

Taking all this into account, one might be tempted to ask why anyone in their right mind or with even an ounce of humanity and compassion would allow themselves to be recruited, and why those who know better would choose to uphold the controversial views and problematic policies of such a duplicitous administration. Then again, in light of the state's tyrannical control of its citizens, allies, and its factitious reputation, one must also realize that pledging to fight this uphill battle was easier said than done. In the following passage, Bezmenov discussed the reasoning behinds his actions: "There really is no simple answer. For one thing, a Soviet journalist cannot simply say 'no' to the KGB. If he wants to remain alive, free, pursue his career, and travel abroad, he...must cooperate with the KGB or suffer the consequences. Secondly, apart from monetary and material gains, a Soviet journalist [hired] by the KGB [rarely gets the chance] to become important in his own country, and in 1965, the USSR was still my country. Many of my colleagues...naively [believed] that they could promote themselves to higher positions of power while maintaining their secretly kept moral principles and disguising their actual disgust of the system."

The "monetary and material gains" referenced by Bezmenov were naturally the most attractive of all the incentives, as the rest barely qualified as such. Novosti-employed journalists were guaranteed to live among the elite, as they were each gifted a fully-furnished apartment, a *dacha* (country house), a private car, and round-trip tickets for international flights, all fully paid for by the Soviet government. Russians who were privileged enough to travel overseas were given the exclusive opportunity to see what life was like outside of the USSR. Those in governmental fields were also free to partake in alcohol, illicit drugs, sexual trysts, and other forms of "Western" decadence unpunished, and they could purchase imported goods tax-free. Moreover, aside from the chance to hobnob with top-level Soviet dignitaries, which elevated the prospect of career advancement, Novosti propagandists were often given clearance to unadulterated military and political intelligence, as well as uncensored domestic and international news.

In the late spring of 1966, Bezmenov and his colleagues were made to work on a collaborative project with *Look* magazine, a popular biweekly publication based in Iowa most known for its phenomenal photographs and illustrations, courtesy of artists such as Norman Rockwell and Stanley Kubrick. Along with those, the magazine also included general-interest articles. A dozen American journalists had been appointed to take a trip to the USSR and cover the 50th anniversary of the October Uprising for the special October 1967 issue, which was to be entitled "Russia Today." Bezmenov later slammed the issue in question as "a package of lies...from the first page to the last page, [containing] propaganda cliches which were presented to American readers as opinions and deductions of American journalists." It was a compilation of primarily laudatory, upbeat content loaded with meaningless buzz words and just a sprinkling of feeble criticisms, partnered with photographs showcasing the USSR's advanced road systems, state-of-the-art technology, and happy-go-lucky youth sporting stylish bikinis and liberal, Western-style fashion.

The following excerpt was perhaps the most telling piece of evidence that pointed to the *Look* reporters' collusion with the Soviet state, be it premeditated or unconscious, as the author confidently vouched for the authenticity of the party's approval ratings: "If an honest democratic election were held in the Soviet Union today...the Communist Party would win. This is not a speculation. It is a conclusion based on on-the-spot observation and interviews by 10 *Look* editors and photographers whose journeys through the Soviet Union for this issue totaled more than a year..."

Like all other domestic and foreign reporters cleared to work in Moscow, the *Look* journalists were each given 25-page-long "backgrounders" prepared by Novosti, which outlined taboo topics, terms, and phrases, as well as statistics, key words, and opinions that they would like highlighted. Only those who consented to the state's censorship conditions were eligible for visas. These guidelines and restrictions, which also applied to foreign journalists based in the USSR, were nothing new and had been enforced since Stalin's dictatorship. William Henry Chamberlin, the Moscow correspondent for the *Christian Science Monitor*, poetically described the conditional relationship between the Kremlin and the foreign press: "[A foreign reporter] works under a Sword of Damocles – the threat of expulsion from the country or of the refusal of permission to re-enter it." Cooperative foreign journalists were also entitled to perks such as free flats, cars, and other lavish gifts, as well as highly sought-after interviews with upper-level politicians.

In early 1969, Bezmenov was stationed in New Delhi, whereupon he was promoted to press officer and public relations agent, working out of the local Soviet embassy. About a month or so after his arrival, the CPSU clandestinely installed a new department in every Soviet embassy worldwide, which they called the "Research and Counter-Propaganda Group." Bezmenov served as the deputy chief of the RCPG in India, answering directly to Valeri Neyev, a respected commentator and contributor of various Novosti publications, most notably the *Novosti Observer*. His principal duty was to collect and organize intel of military and political value, survey data regarding public opinion on India and the Soviet Union, and invasive personal information about local figures – from Parliament members and military officials to revered intellectuals, popular journalists, affluent socialites, successful industrialists, and celebrities – that could be used as bargaining chips or blackmail material. These tips were provided by both local civilians and government agents, who were showered with monetary rewards, tax-free alcohol, and complimentary tickets to the USSR. Snitches in academic fields were often invited to sham conventions and presented with bogus literary medals and peace plaques, which came with princely cash prizes.

Occasionally, Bezmenov himself was sent out in the field. He claimed that he had been ordered to pose as a beginner yogi looking to experiment with Transcendental Meditation at the infamous ashram of Maharishi Mahesh Yogi. The actual purpose of his undercover work was to investigate the premises, explore the rumors about the infiltration of a CIA spy ring, and to analyze Mahesh's rapidly growing and surprisingly star-studded following, which included the Beatles, Beach Boys, Clint Eastwood, Deepak Chopra, and billionaire tobacco heiress Doris Duke. Bezmenov explained, "The KGB was even curious about [Mahesh]...[The] Beatles...Mia Farrow and other useful idiots from Hollywood visited his school and they returned to [the] United States absolutely zonked out of their minds with marijuana, hashish, and crazy ideas of meditation...Obviously [the] KGB was very fascinated with such a beautiful school, such a brainwashing center for stupid Americans."

Maharishi

Bezmenov's joy at reuniting with his beloved India was quickly smothered when the truth behind the KGB's compulsive data collection dawned on him, or more precisely, what the Kremlin had accomplished and planned to accomplish with their intel. He remembered how he had stumbled upon a report about a 26-day-long siege now known as the "Hue Massacre" while rifling through a stack of USA Information Service documents that had been leaked to the Soviets. The occupied city of Hue, situated in central Vietnam, had been subjugated by the communist Viet Cong and North Vietnamese Army on January 30, 1969, and when the US Army reclaimed Hue on February 26, they unearthed clusters of mass graves containing a dizzying 2,800 (some estimates say up to 5,700) civilians accused of sympathizing with the Saigon government and being "Pro-American." These civilians – priests, schoolteachers, and working men and women, even children – were slaughtered in ghastly fashion. Those who were shot were considered the lucky ones. Others were hog-tied with electric wire and gagged, then pummeled to death with crowbars and shovels. Some corpses, according to Foreign Service Officer Douglas Pike, were "contorted but without wounds, an indication that they were buried alive." Even more disturbing yet, all those executed had reportedly been rounded up and exterminated in one night.

Bezmenov, who had no previous knowledge of this tragedy, became even more concerned when he learned how the guerrilla forces had managed to track down all these dissidents in such a short stretch of time. Informers at the Soviet embassy in Hanoi had allegedly been gathering and feeding intel to the Vietnamese communists for months or even years before they went on the offensive. Bezmenov noted, "The Communists filed every bit of information: addresses, personal habits, political affiliations, expressed ideas, unexpressed thoughts revealed in informal and private conversations, even the names and addresses of relatives, friends, even lovers and mistresses of the future victims of 'liberation.'"

Bezmenov's entire world came crashing down like a ton of bricks, triggered by an avalanche of revelations, the shattering of previously held delusions and denials, and an overwhelming sense of remorse. It was supposedly then that it occurred to him the intel amassed by his department had been or had the potential to be used in the oppression, persecution, and genocidal slaughter of thousands, maybe even millions of innocents in India, a nation near and dear to his heart. He later admitted, "Since I fell in love with India, I developed something which by KGB standards is an extremely dangerous thing. It's called 'split loyalty': when an agent likes a country of assignment more than his own country. I literally fell in love with this beautiful country, a country of great contrasts, but also great humility, great tolerance, and philosophical and intellectual freedoms." The Soviets' camaraderie with India had nothing to do with the pursuit of peace, progress, or solidarity; rather, they sought to impose upon the Indians "a new type of colonialism" through extortion, exploitation, brazen untruths, and the suppression of free speech.

Bezmenov's distress was heightened further when he confronted the sinister reality of the KGB-operated universities, the Institute of Oriental Languages included. Apart from the grooming of KGB agents or informants, institutions such as the Lumumba Friendship University and other similar learning and research centers in Crimea and Tashkent, which marketed themselves as schools that aimed to provide higher education to underprivileged students from Third World nations, were training centers for future founders and commanders of Kremlin-sponsored "liberation movements." Bezmenov claimed that the founding fathers of the Mukti Fauj, the forerunner of the *Mukti Bahini* (or Freedom Fighters) had attended one of the aforementioned KGB-run universities. These Bangladeshi guerrilla fighters robbed banks, raided warehouses and commercial ships, ransacked the mansions of wealthy businessmen, attempted to destabilize power plants and railway companies, and murdered 100,000-150,000 Biharis (up to 20% of the Bihari population) and non-Bengalis throughout the 1970s.

Bezmenov spent the following months plunging further down this bottomless rabbit hole. His self-assigned research revealed that the KGB had unleashed thousands of undercover KGB agents in East Pakistan, where they were tasked with aiding insurgents in raising a rebellion. All the while, they were using India as a "jumping board" to seize control of the province. Bezmenov insisted, "I saw myself, thousands of so-called 'students' traveling through India to

East Pakistan through the territory of India. The Indian government pretended not to see what was going on."

In December 1969, a close colleague approached him with what he perceived to be indisputable, concrete proof of Soviet involvement in Indian terrorism. His colleague, who had been stationed in the Soviet embassy in Calcutta, had been hitting the bottle after office hours the previous evening and had gotten completely hammered. In his drunken stupor, he was unable to locate the bathroom and wandered around aimlessly searching for a spot to empty his bladder. He wound up in the basement storage room, which had incidentally been left unlocked, and after he urinated, he came upon a heap of boxes bearing the label: "Printed Matter to Dhaka University."

Wondering what kind of reading material Novosti had prepared for the students at one of the top universities in Dacca, the capital of East Pakistan, he unfolded the lids of the boxes and peered inside. He expected to see reams of familiarly-worded documents and pamphlets, and maybe a few morbid chuckles from the often ludicrous claims made by the state's premier propagandists. To his horror, he found himself staring down at mountains of Kalashnikov AK-47s and bundles of ammunition.

Bezmenov was beside himself with rage, resentment, and contrition. He had reached his breaking point, and he vowed he could no longer in good conscience continue to work for a system as corrupt, deceptive, and depraved as the Soviet state.

A Changed Man

"Whether I scare some people or not, I don't give a hoot. If you're not scared by now, nothing can scare you." – Yuri Bezmenov

Bezmenov's decision to cut ties with the Soviet Union was not one made lightly. He was, more than anything, haunted by the possibility if not outright certainty of retribution from the KGB. He further accepted the fact that he had no one to trust or rely on but himself, and he had to be willing to jeopardize his own safety to defect. Put simply, if he was apprehended, he would most definitely be shipped off to the *gulag* or disappear without a trace. At the same time, he found it supremely difficult to come to terms with the reality that his departure would mean endangering the lives of his loved ones and colleagues back home. He wrestled with his feelings for a while, full of excitement, giddy optimism, and redemption, which conflicted with his blinding guilt, paralyzing fear, and intermittent cold feet.

In the end, it all boiled down to the one thing: it was his incontrovertible duty to defect from the Soviet Union, no matter the cost, if putting an end to the Kremlin's atrocities was what he truly desired. It was only outside the Iron Curtain that he could warn the world and bring about real, lasting change.

Bezmenov hatched an escape plan built on all the tricks and maneuvers he had picked up from his decades of training, one that his mentors would never see coming. On February 8, 1970, Bezmenov invited two of his colleagues to catch a movie at a nearby cinema. The threesome settled on a showing of the 1967 American neo-noir thriller *The Incident,* starring Tony Musante, Ed McMahon, Beau Bridges, and Martin Sheen in his feature-film debut. Around 10 minutes before the previews were set to kick off, the intentionally tardy Bezmenov urged his colleagues to go on in without him, as he had not yet purchased his ticket for the sold-out screening. He claimed he would purchase one from a scalper hawking said tickets in the back alley. That was the last his colleagues saw of him.

Bezmenov snuck into a public bathroom and began his transformation. He slipped into a gaudy, oversized tie-dye *kameez* embellished with fringes and beads, as well as a pair of jeans, and removed his loafers. He then donned a scraggly, waist-length wig, pasted on a fake beard, and rubbed some cannabis buds on his clothes to complete the illusion. In his new wardrobe, Bezmenov was indistinguishable from the thousands of new-age, hashish-smoking American "peaceniks," mainly travelers and exchange students, that had swarmed India in recent years. To avoid detection by local policemen, he even adopted the stereotypical "hippie" lingo. He had even gone so far as to scout out common hippie hangouts, and he learned the different ingestion techniques for a variety of substances for research purposes in the weeks leading up to his escape.

His camouflage operation was a raving success, for he managed to enter Athens unnoticed. Meanwhile, his superiors quickly noticed his absence and promptly sounded the alarms. Indian publications nationwide reported on the missing Russian diplomat and offered 2,000 rupees for any information that could lead to his whereabouts.

In time, news of this intriguing turn of events swiftly made its away across the Atlantic. American journalists surmised that the diplomat had defected and was now on the lam. When these reporters approached their Soviet sources for comment, a spokesperson appointed by the KGB downplayed the situation, describing Bezmenov as a disgruntled, low-level, unimportant clerical worker whose absence, while disheartening, would not be missed.

In Athens, Bezmenov teamed up with tight-lipped CIA agents and endured four months of extensive background checks and intensive interrogations. Only when the asylum seeker gained the trust of the CIA agents did they arrange for him a flight to Germany. He holed up in Munich, where he was placed under the protection of Munich-based CIA agents for a few weeks, and he was finally flown out to Canada in late July. Humiliated by their inability to locate what they referred to as a menial "clerical worker," the Soviet embassy at New Delhi announced that the missing diplomat had been kidnapped and most likely murdered by a rogue group of anti-Communist revolutionaries. They went so far as to publicly reward an undisclosed amount to Bezmenov's son in restitution.

Bezmenov, as advised by the CIA and Canadian Royal Mounted Police, assumed a brand-new identity: Thomas David Schuman. It was imperative that he steer clear of any unwanted attention for obvious reasons, and as such, he made certain to keep a low profile, at least for a few years. The 31-year-old returned to school, studying history and political science at the University of Toronto for four semesters. To pay the bills, he juggled a few jobs, working as a fieldhand at an obscure farm in Ontario and moonlighting as a laundry truck driver for three years. He then landed a job as a Russian language instructor and literature professor at a local school.

Bezmenov eventually began his whistleblowing campaign in the summer of 1973, during which he applied for and secured a post at the Canadian Broadcasting Corporation in Montreal. He was assigned to the CBC's International Service department, and in addition to announcing and producing, he wrote the segments that would be broadcast in the Soviet Union. Life, it seemed, was going swell. It was during this time that he met a Canadian woman known only as "Tess," who married him. The couple had a daughter named Tanya and a son named Jonathan.

Unfortunately, his dream job at the CBC, which provided him with the stability and purpose he had so longed for, was short-lived. He had hoped that his scandalous stories of the crooked Soviet and foreign media, the diabolical crimes and unethical activities of the KGB, and the Kremlin's future plans for subversion, along with his incessant pestering of the CIA, would trigger some kind of mass awakening. In 1975, for example, he claimed that Novosti had sold 16 articles, rife with propaganda and flat-out lies, about the Soviet Union to *Encyclopedia Britannica*, which rambled on about the USSR's picturesque landscapes and historical landmarks and the stellar work of their admirable youth groups and political organizations, but left out their aggressive takeover of Asian, Baltic, and Eastern European states, as well as the mysterious disappearance of 40% of the USSR's native populations. Bezmenov railed at the callous indifference demonstrated by his listeners and Western leaders, complaining, "No one wanted either my information or to open up their eyes. People prefer to remain comfortably, blissfully unaware of things unpleasant."

He claimed that he had appealed to his direct superior for help, who, to his consternation, plainly stated that he "did not give a damn" about his woes and provided him with a sobering reality check. Western leaders were the first to advocate for peace talks and war-ending negotiations, but they were every bit as corrupt as the Soviet state, for they were only interested in resolving disputes and correcting injustices when it was convenient for them, or more importantly, when it directly affected them.

As one might have expected, KGB surveillance agents charged with monitoring all domestic and international televised and radio broadcasts eventually uncovered the true identity of Thomas Schuman. In 1976, Alexandr Yakovlev, the USSR Ambassador to Canada, lodged a lengthy complaint against Bezmenov and the CBC's Soviet segment, which soon landed on the desk of Prime Minister Pierre Trudeau. Yakovlev was extremely friendly with the prime minister, so much so that the latter named his second son, Alexandre, after the Soviet ambassador. Bezmenov was ultimately reprimanded for his supposedly false and inflammatory anti-Soviet comments and forced to resign.

Yakovlev

Trudeau

According to Bezmenov, his misery was compounded by subtle, but very real death threats from Canadian Soviet embassy officials, who warned him to "cross the street carefully," given the "heavy traffic in Quebec." He was, however, more irritated than he was frightened by these thinly-veiled threats, as he was intimately familiar with KGB intimidation tactics. He, too, was a fast driver, Bezmenov retorted, and sarcastically invited these officials to swing by his home for a visit any time, where he would happily show them his hidden stockpile of Kalashnikov machine guns.

Feeling demoralized and betrayed by Trudeau and his bosses at CBC, who, in his opinion, "behaved in a very cowardly way unbecoming of a free country like Canada," Bezmenov took matters into his own hands by moving to Los Angeles in the late '70s or early '80s. Once he got there, he became a freelance journalist and political analyst, regularly contributing to publications such as the *World Information Network* and *Almanac Panorama*. In his spare time, he delivered lectures, appeared in hour-long interviews, and authored a number of books under the name Thomas Schuman, including *Love Letter to America* (1984), *Black is Beautiful* (1985), *No "Novosti" is Good News* (1985), and *World Thought Police* (1986).

Slowly, but surely, Bezmenov began to attract media attention, as well as a steady following that hung on his every word. At a lecture in the winter of 1983, he insinuated that the tragic crash of Korean Air Lines Flight 007 that September, which had been downed by Soviet missiles that killed all 269 passengers and crew members, was no accident. The Soviet military pilots who intercepted the passenger jet insisted that they had been unable to establish contact with the KAL pilots and therefore determined it to be an unauthorized spy plane that had entered Russian airspace. In truth, according to Bezmenov, the Soviets were well-aware that the plane was scheduled to enter Russian territory and had deliberately shot down the plane in a bid to assassinate Larry McDonald, the Democratic and stalwartly anti-communist House Representative of Georgia's 7th Congressional District.

In an interview with the *Washington Times* in January of 1984, Bezmenov petitioned President Reagan to revoke the visas and unrestricted traveling privileges granted to Soviet journalists and tourists who were traveling to Los Angeles for the 1984 Summer Olympics. An extract from the article, written by George Archibald, told readers, "Mr. Schuman said 'at least 75% of Soviet journalists are KGB members whose assignments during the Olympics will include spying, subversion, and recruitment of agents to buy, steal, or search out US high-technology secrets.' He said the administration should also turn down 25 Aeroflot planes in Los Angeles...as they are 'equipped for aerial spying and provide better control against possible athletic defections'...[and to] dock a large cruise ship in Los Angeles Harbor...[which as] a 'piece of soviet territory [is] not subject to normal search procedures...[and would contain] 300 KGB agents...[who will be] busy vacuuming the air waves to record military communications, private telephone conversations, police arrangements, and federal security strategies'..."

Bezmenov's most famous disclosures were first publicized in an interview that same year with the illustrious and controversial author G. Edward Griffin, which was broadcast with the sensational title: "Soviet Subversion of the Free World Press." The broadcast exposed all sorts of dirty secrets, including: the USSR's dark, symbiotic relationship with its allies; the state's complete lack of journalistic integrity; the *gulags*, which he claimed was home to 25-30 million Soviet prisoners at any given time; and the virulent disinformation spread by state propagandists, including a rumor that condoms led to the proliferation of HIV, among other Soviet secrets. He also divulged the Soviet Union's plans for ideological subversion, which occurred in four stages. It was naive of the public to believe that the Soviet administration invested the bulk of its time in conducting espionage, as "85% [of their time, money, and manpower] is spent on a slow process...[they called] ideological subversion, active measures, or psychological warfare."

The following passages, taken from Bezmenov's *Love Letter to America* and the transcript of his 1984 interview, are a condensed summary of these four stages: "Stage one: demoralization – It takes about 15 to 20 years to demoralize a nation...the minimum number of years needed to 'educate' one generation of students in a target country...To be successful, the process of subversion [at this stage] must be always and only a two-way street which means that the target nation must be made a recipient – passive or active – of the ideas of the subverter...In other words, Marxism-Leninism ideology is being pumped into...at least three generations of American students without being challenged...[You can see the result in] most of the people who graduated in the '60s...Drop-outs or half-baked intellectuals are now occupying the positions of power in the government, civil service, business, mass media, and educational system. You are stuck with them...You cannot change their mind even if you expose them to authentic information..."

The second stage, which was "destabilization," required a period of anywhere between two to five years:

"Here, the efforts of [the] subverter narrow down to the 'essentials': the internal power structures of a target nation, the nation's foreign relations, economy, and 'social fiber.'...The first symptom of instability is expressed as the desire of the population to bring to power politicians and parties who are charismatic, act like good 'caretakers,' and promise more...job 'security' [instead of increased defense against external and foreign enemies], 'free' social services,' and other 'pleasure strokes' provided by 'Big Brother.' By concentrating the attention of a nation on short-term solutions and 'improvements,' such irresponsible politicians simply procrastinate on facing 'the moment of truth,' when the nation will have to pay a much higher price for...bringing [back] the stability of the country and restoring moral fiber.

"With the final destruction of the free bargaining process...the State...functions more and more 'in cahoots' with mega-monopolies and monopolized labor unions. The famous 'division of powers' no longer governs the judicial, legislative, and executive lines, but rather is replaced by bureaucracy in government, bureaucracy in business, and bureaucracy in labor."

The third stage, labeled "crisis," required a much shorter timeframe: two months to half a year:

"At this third stage of subversion, you will have all your American 'radicals' and Soviet 'sleeper' agents springing into action, trying to 'seize power as quickly and ruthlessly as possible.'...If all the previous stages of Soviet subversion have been successfully completed...the majority of Americans will be so totally confused that they may even welcome 'strong' leaders who 'know how to talk to the Russians.'

"...A forceful change of the US system may...be accomplished through a civil war or internal revolution, and a physical military invasion by the USSR may not even have to take place at all. But change it will be...with all the familiar attributes of Soviet 'progress' being instituted such as nationalization of vital industries, the reduction of the 'private sector' of the economy...the redistribution of wealth, and a massive propaganda campaign..."

Last, but not least, was stage four, dauntingly entitled "normalization." It claimed:

"[T]here will arise pockets of resistance shortly after the takeover consisting of the 'enemy classes and counter-revolutionaries' who will physically resist the new system...Reforms of the security agencies...by the new government may lead to a situation of 'split loyalties' among law enforcement officers and render the majority of the population defenseless...At this point, to avoid 'the bloodshed,' the subverter moves to normalization...the vanquished country...brought by force into the normal state of socialism: namely, subjugation.

"This is when...you will start seeing 'friendly' Soviet soldiers in the streets of [American] cities working together with American soldiers and the 'new' police force to 'restore law and order.' Very soon your yesterday's American...'do-gooders' who were working...to [effect] progress...will find themselves in prisons and...concentration camps. Many of them will be executed...No more criticism of the State; the Press will obediently censor itself...You will now have the opportunity to 'enjoy' exactly the same life as the Vietnamese, Cambodians, Angolans, and Nicaraguans..."

The details of Bezmenov's final days, much like his childhood and formative years, are few and far between. His marriage apparently dissolved with an amicable divorce in 1989, after which he moved to Ontario, while his wife and children remained in Montreal. He continued to write a few articles for national publications here and there, and in early 1991, he acquired a post as a professor of international relations at the University of Windsor.

The following Christmas, he flew to Montreal to celebrate the holiday with his ex-wife and children. Bezmenov had lost quite a bit of weight and was somewhat haggard, appearing visibly ill. As if he had known what was coming, he seemed determined to spend what little quality time he had left with his 14-year-old daughter and 10-year-old son.

His death was reported across Windsor newspapers, including the *Windsor Star*, on January 6, 1993. Bezmenov had apparently succumbed to complications following a severe heart attack at Grace Hospital, which experts suggested may have been brought on by his alcoholism. He was 54.

To this day, particularly with Bezmenov's recent resurgence in popularity, whether or not the KGB defector can be considered a reputable source remains a bitter bone of contention. Was he a flawed, but valiant hero who risked his life to unmask the dangerously devious Soviet administration and its schemes? Or was he, as the Russians suggested, a deeply unhappy and malcontent civil servant with an inferiority complex who, at one point, compared himself to Winston Smith from George Orwell's *Nineteen Eighty-Four* and was hell-bent on securing his 15 minutes of fame?

Bezmenov was no stranger to the controversy. Indeed, he predicted the lasting skepticism that continues to surround his motives. Fittingly, Bezmenov provided his own best defense: "What do I get for defecting from the winning side (the Soviets)...and joining the losers? I hope I don't have to tell you that at least a dozen countries have succumbed to the Communists since my defection...Dear friends, I have gained nothing materially from my defection. What I have gained is a firm commitment to the United States as the last real frontier of freedom. [Our] country will be the last to be 'liberated' by Marxists, socialists, and domestic 'do-gooders'. If the 'liberationists' succeed in bringing their 'New Order' to America, chances are, you and I will meet in front of a firing squad – or worse, in a 're-education' forced labor camp in the Alaskan Peoples Democratic Republic..."

What one makes of that is their prerogative.

Online Resources

Other books about 20th century history by Charles River Editors

Other books about Russian history by Charles River Editors

Other books about Bezmenov on Amazon

Bibliography

Abramowitz, K. (2020, August 2). It's time to rediscover KGB defector Yuri Bezmenov. Retrieved December 5, 2020, from https://www.jns.org/opinion/its-time-to-rediscover-kgb-defector-yuri-bezmenov/

Applebaum, A. (2017, October 13). How Stalin Hid Ukraine's Famine From the World. Retrieved December 5, 2020, from https://www.theatlantic.com/international/archive/2017/10/red-famine-anne-applebaum-ukraine-soviet-union/542610/

Ash, L. (2015, January 29). How Russia outfoxes its enemies. Retrieved December 5, 2020, from https://www.bbc.com/news/magazine-31020283

Assadollahi, S. (2020, November 2). The "Friendship" between Pierre Elliott Trudeau and the Soviets — a historic Fact! Retrieved December 5, 2020, from https://shabnamassadollahi.medium.com/the-friendship-between-pierre-elliott-trudeau-and-the-soviets-a-historic-fact-a594de4bd729

Binayak, P. (2018, March 13). 11 Great Inventions We Can Thank India For. Retrieved December 5, 2020, from https://theculturetrip.com/asia/india/articles/11-great-inventions-we-can-thank-india-for/

Bose, A. (2018, February 23). When Indian parliamentarians saw a CIA plot in the Beatles' stay at Maharishi Mahesh Yogi's ashram. Retrieved December 5, 2020, from https://scroll.in/magazine/869696/when-indian-parliamentarians-saw-a-cia-plot-in-the-beatles-stay-at-maharishi-mahesh-yogis-ashram

Bryce, T. (2012, April 25). The Four Steps for American Subversion. Retrieved December 5, 2020, from https://patch.com/florida/dunedin/bp--the-four-steps-for-american-subversion-5985fc5a

Byrd, M. (2020, August 20). Call of Duty Black Ops: Cold War – Who Is Yuri Bezmenov? Retrieved December 5, 2020, from https://www.denofgeek.com/games/call-of-duty-black-ops-cold-war-yuri-bezmenov-ezplained/

Campbell, H. (2009, January 19). Mytishchi. Retrieved December 5, 2020, from https://www.britannica.com/place/Mytishchi

Cesereanu, R. (2006). Portrait of the Torturer in the 20th Century. Retrieved December 5, 2020, from http://www.columbia.edu/cu/ece/research/intermarium/vol10no1/Portrait%20of%20the%20Torturer%20in%20the%2020th%20Century.pdf

Chhibber, M. (2018, October 2). K. Kamaraj: The southern stalwart who gave India two PMs. Retrieved December 5, 2020, from https://theprint.in/politics/k-kamaraj-the-southern-stalwart-who-gave-india-two-pms/127890/

Cohen, D. (2013, August 14). 10 famous/infamous whistleblowers. Retrieved December 5, 2020, from https://www.politico.com/gallery/2013/08/10-famous-infamous-whistleblowers-001083?slide=0

Cull, N. J., Gatov, V., Pomerantsev, P., Applebaum, A., & Shawcross, A. (2017, October). Soviet Subversion, Disinformation and Propaganda: How the West Fought Against it. Retrieved December 5, 2020, from https://www.lse.ac.uk/iga/assets/documents/arena/2018/Jigsaw-Soviet-Subversion-Disinformation-and-Propaganda-Final-Report.pdf

Editors, A. D. (2014, October 10). KAL 007: A Targeted Assassination? Retrieved December 5, 2020, from https://adst.org/2014/10/kal-007-a-targeted-assassination/

Editors, C. G. (2010, August 24). KGB Defector Blames '60s Activists for Soviet Success. Retrieved December 5, 2020, from https://www.cia.gov/library/readingroom/docs/CIA-RDP90-00552R000605880003-3.pdf

Editors, C. G. (2017). Who Killed Krivitzky? Retrieved December 5, 2020, from https://www.cia.gov/library/readingroom/docs/CIA-RDP75-00149R000400430018-5.pdf

Editors, C. L. (2017). Yuri Bezmenov: Lecture on Subversion (1983). Retrieved December 5, 2020, from https://cosmolearning.org/documentaries/yuri-bezmenov-lecture-on-subversion-1983/6/

Editors, C. N. (2020, November 2). Edward Snowden Fast Facts. Retrieved December 5, 2020, from https://edition.cnn.com/2013/09/11/us/edward-snowden-fast-facts/index.html

Editors, D. M. (2017, October 16). Marxism and Gandhian perspective of Sumitranandan Pant. Retrieved December 5, 2020, from https://doonmozaic.com/marxism-gandhian-sumitranandan-pant/

Editors, D. T. (2008, March 12). Borodin, Norman Mikhailovich. Retrieved December 5, 2020, from http://documentstalk.com/wp/borodin-norman-mikhailovich/

Editors, E. C. (2020, November 24). Kurbsky, Andrei Mikhailovich. Retrieved December 5, 2020, from https://www.encyclopedia.com/history/encyclopedias-almanacs-transcripts-and-maps/kurbsky-andrei-mikhailovich

Editors, F. 2. (2020, February 24). Julian Assange: World's most-wanted whistleblower back in spotlight. Retrieved December 5, 2020, from https://www.france24.com/en/20200224-julian-assange-world-s-most-wanted-whistleblower-back-in-spotlight

Editors, F. D. (2018, October 20). How the USSR created a myth about Americans intentionally infecting Europe with the Colorado potato beetle. Retrieved December 5, 2020, from https://www.forumdaily.com/en/kak-sozdayutsya-mify-amerikancy-namerenno-zarazili-evropu-koloradskim-zhukom

Editors, F. S. (2015). The Words of the Reverend Schuman: Stages of Subversion. Retrieved December 5, 2020, from http://faktasiden.no/dokumenter/kgb-hjernevasking.pdf

Editors, G. N. (2020, June 5). Who is Behind the Riots? How to Move Forward? Retrieved December 5, 2020, from https://gnews.org/223314/

Editors, H. C. (2020, February 24). Mass graves discovered in Hue. Retrieved December 5, 2020, from https://www.history.com/this-day-in-history/mass-graves-discovered-in-hue

Editors, I. A. (2017, June). Ambassador Pankaj Saran's visit to Chechnya Republic. Retrieved December 5, 2020, from https://indianembassy-moscow.gov.in/70-years-of-india-russia-relations-a-historic-milestone.php

Editors, I. A. (2018). Full text of "Bezmenov: LOVE LETTER TO AMERICA". Retrieved December 5, 2020, from https://archive.org/stream/BezmenovLoveLetterToAmerica/YuriBezmenov-LoveLetterToAmerica_djvu.txt

Editors, I. A. (2018). Full text of "Yuri Bezmenov: World Thought Police". Retrieved December 5, 2020, from https://archive.org/stream/Yuri-Bezmenov_World-Thought-Police/Yuri-Bezmenov_World-Thought-Police_djvu.txt

Editors, I. O. (2019). History of the Institute of Oriental Studies of the Russian Academy of Sciences - 19th Century. Retrieved December 5, 2020, from http://www.ivran.ru/en/history-of-the-institute

Editors, M. (2019, October 16). The Yuri Bezmenov Conundrum. Retrieved December 5, 2020, from https://medium.com/@uspatriotdude2/the-yuri-bezmenov-conundrum-210e44b401e9

Editors, M. V. (2018, September 21). Urban Naxals and their KGB roots. Retrieved December 5, 2020, from https://myvoice.opindia.com/2018/09/urban-naxals-and-their-kgb-roots/

Editors, N. B. (2014, May 26). Who Is Edward Snowden, the Man Who Spilled the NSA's Secrets? Retrieved December 5, 2020, from https://www.nbcnews.com/feature/edward-snowden-interview/who-edward-snowden-man-who-spilled-nsas-secrets-n114861

Editors, N. S. (2008, February 6). Maharishi Mahesh Yogi, 91, Guru to the Stars. Retrieved December 5, 2020, from https://www.nysun.com/obituaries/maharishi-mahesh-yogi-91-guru-to-the-stars/70827/

Editors, N. T. (1971, November 9). Terrorism In Dacca. Retrieved December 5, 2020, from https://www.nytimes.com/1971/11/09/archives/terrorism-in-dacca.html

Editors, O. I. (2020, June 19). Former KGB agent Yuri Bezmenov exposes the four stages of a Communist takeover of a country in rare 1984 interview. Retrieved December 5, 2020, from https://www.opindia.com/2020/06/former-kgb-agent-yuri-bezmenov-exposes-the-four-stages-of-a-communist-takeover-of-a-country-in-rare-1984-interview/

Editors, R. B. (2018, September 10). 15 Soviet anti-American posters from the Cold War. Retrieved December 5, 2020, from https://www.rbth.com/history/329103-15-soviet-anti-american-posters

Editors, T. G. (2020). Kurbish years of life. Andrey Kurbsky. Retrieved December 5, 2020, from https://tugulympu.ru/en/kurbskii-gody-zhizni-andrei-kurbskii-biografiya-knyazya-v-rechi-pospolitoi/

Editors, T. R. (2019, April 30). "High-ranking defector": What role in voivode Andrey Kurbsky played in national history. Retrieved December 5, 2020, from https://www.tellerreport.com/tech/--%E2%80%9Chigh-ranking-defector%E2%80%9D--what-role-in-voivode-andrey-kurbsky-played-in-national-history-.S1G8XiBoV.html

Editors, T. T. (2013). The Khrushchev "thaw" (1953-1964). Retrieved December 5, 2020, from http://www.territoryterror.org.ua/en/history/1953-1964/

Editors, U. C. (2020, July 14). Bezmenov's Steps. Retrieved December 5, 2020, from https://unintendedconsequenc.es/bezmenovs-steps/

Editors, W. S. (2015, May 3). Soviet Defector Held Passion for Homeland (Archive) - Windsor Star. Retrieved December 5, 2020, from https://drive.google.com/file/d/0B7dmym4cK6ABRU5lNlZpYVlGVEE/view

Editors, W. T. (2010, June 24). Ex-Spy Urges Curbing Soviets at Olympics. Retrieved December 5, 2020, from https://www.cia.gov/library/readingroom/docs/CIA-RDP90-00806R000200860037-5.pdf

Egerov, B. (2018, March 19). 5 most impressive and important drills of the Soviet Army. Retrieved December 5, 2020, from https://www.rbth.com/history/327837-5-most-impressive-soviet-drills

Elliott, J. K. (2018, June 9). Theatricality and deception: How Russia uses 'maskirovka' to shake the world. Retrieved December 5, 2020, from https://globalnews.ca/news/4260938/russia-strategy-maskirovka-military-politics-putin/

Ermolaev, S. (2017, March 29). The Formation and Evolution of the Soviet Union's Oil and Gas Dependence. Retrieved December 5, 2020, from https://carnegieendowment.org/2017/03/29/formation-and-evolution-of-soviet-union-s-oil-and-gas-dependence-pub-68443

Fleming, R. (1989, Summer). Lenin's Conception of Socialism: Learning from the early experiences of the world's first socialist revolution. Retrieved December 5, 2020, from https://www.marxists.org/history/erol/ncm-7/lenin-socialism.htm

Glass, A. (2017, September 1). Rep. McDonald dies when Soviets shoot down Boeing 747, Sept. 1, 1983. Retrieved December 5, 2020, from https://www.politico.com/story/2017/09/01/rep-mcdonald-dies-when-soviets-shoot-down-boeing-747-sept-1-1983-242130

Harding, L. (2020, October 24). Marxist Media Management. Retrieved December 5, 2020, from https://fcpp.org/2020/10/24/marxist-media-management/

Ioffe, J. (2017, October 21). The History of Russian Involvement in America's Race Wars. Retrieved December 5, 2020, from https://www.theatlantic.com/international/archive/2017/10/russia-facebook-race/542796/

Loushnikova, E. (2015, January 13). Comrade Stalin's secret prison. Retrieved December 5, 2020, from https://www.opendemocracy.net/en/odr/comrade-stalins-secret-prison/

Lyons, J. (2018, August 3). Mammoth Military Exercises of the Soviet Union with Video. Retrieved December 5, 2020, from https://www.warhistoryonline.com/instant-articles/large-military-exercises-soviet.html

Mishra, A. (2017, April 30). A Russian spy exposes the "Breaking India" conspiracy of elite universities, left parties and Media. Retrieved December 5, 2020, from https://tfipost.com/2017/04/russian-spy-yuri-bezmenov-conspiracy-01/

Monsen, L. (2020, April 29). America sent gear to the USSR to help win World War II. Retrieved December 5, 2020, from https://share.america.gov/america-sent-equipment-to-soviet-union-in-world-war-ii/

Offner, A. A. (2011, February 17). President Truman and the Origins of the Cold War. Retrieved December 5, 2020, from http://www.bbc.co.uk/history/worldwars/wwtwo/truman_01.shtml

Overdorf, J. (2012, November 28). Archaeologists confirm Indian civilization is 2000 years older than previously believed. Retrieved December 5, 2020, from https://www.pri.org/stories/2012-11-28/archaeologists-confirm-indian-civilization-2000-years-older-previously-believed

Pishchik, B. (2010). Novosti Press Agency. Retrieved December 5, 2020, from https://encyclopedia2.thefreedictionary.com/Novosti+Press+Agency

Ratner, P. (2018, July 18). 34 years ago, a KGB defector chillingly predicted modern America. Retrieved December 5, 2020, from https://bigthink.com/paul-ratner/34-years-ago-a-kgb-defector-described-america-today

Saleem, F., PhD. (2016, March 14). Mukti Bahini, the forgotten terrorists. Retrieved December 5, 2020, from https://www.thenews.com.pk/print/105117-Mukti-Bahini-the-forgotten-terrorists

Sharma, U. (2020, May 20). Sumitranandan Pant, the beloved Hindi poet inspired by Lakshman and Napoleon. Retrieved December 5, 2020, from https://theprint.in/features/sumitranandan-pant-the-beloved-hindi-poet-inspired-by-lakshman-and-napoleon/425063/

Showalter, M. (2013, September 20). Six Principles Of Propaganda Lenin Used To Consolidate Power. Retrieved December 5, 2020, from https://www.investors.com/politics/commentary/lenin-used-six-principles-of-propaganda-to-consolidate-control/

Simkin, J. (1997, September). Walter Krivitsky. Retrieved December 5, 2020, from https://spartacus-educational.com/SSkrivitsky.htm

Sloan, J., Jalali, A., Wardak, G., & Giessler, F. (1986, June). SOVIET STYLE WARGAMES. Retrieved December 5, 2020, from https://paxsims.files.wordpress.com/2020/06/soviet-style-wargames-1986-06-ocr-version-2020-06-24.pdf

Stewart, K. G. (2002, January 10). Russian Methods of Interrogating Captured Personnel. Retrieved December 5, 2020, from https://www.cia.gov/library/readingroom/docs/CIA-RDP65-00756R000400030001-4.pdf

Tanabe, J. (2013, April 10). Khrushchev Thaw. Retrieved December 5, 2020, from https://www.newworldencyclopedia.org/entry/Khrushchev_Thaw

West, N. (2009). *The A to Z of Sexspionage*. WI: Scarecrow Press.

White, J. (2019, March 8). Destabilizing a nation. Retrieved December 5, 2020, from https://www.mesabitribune.com/opinion/destabilizing-a-nation/article_3ca6fe84-41f4-11e9-902a-0b851cf34124.html

Free Books by Charles River Editors

We have brand new titles available for free most days of the week. To see which of our titles are currently free, click on this link.

Discounted Books by Charles River Editors

We have titles at a discount price of just 99 cents everyday. To see which of our titles are currently 99 cents, click on this link.

Made in the USA
Middletown, DE
13 June 2023

32524248R00031